FRANCE

Cultures and Costumes Series:

CULTURES AND COSTUMES: SYMBOLS OF THEIR PERIOD

FRANCE

ALYCEN MITCHELL

MASON CREST PUBLISHERS

www.masoncrest.com

Mason Crest Publishers Inc.
370 Reed Road
Broomall, PA 19008
(866) MCP-BOOK (toll free)
www.masoncrest.com

First printing 2002

1 2 3 4 5 6 7 8 9 10

Library of Congress Cataloging-in-Publication Data available

ISBN 1-59084-442-4

Printed and bound in Malaysia

Editorial and design by
Amber Books Ltd.
Bradley's Close
74–77 White Lion Street
London N1 9PF

Project Editor: Marie-Claire Muir
Designer: Hawes Design

Picture Credits:
All pictures courtesy of Amber Books Ltd.

ACKNOWLEDGMENT
For authenticating this book, the Publishers would like to thank
Robert L. Humphrey, Jr., Professor Emeritus of Anthropology,
George Washington University, Washington, D.C.

Contents

France is one of the largest countries in Europe. The English Channel lies to the northwest, the Mediterranean is to the southeast, and over the eastern Alps lie Switzerland and Italy. France also shares borders with Germany, Luxembourg, and Belgium.

Introduction

Nearly every species in the animal kingdom adapts to changes in the environment. To cope with cold weather, the cat adapts by growing a longer coat of fur, the bear hibernates, and birds migrate to a different climatic zone. Only humans use costume and culture—what they have learned through many generations—to adapt to the environment.

The first humans developed their culture by using spears to hunt the bear, knives and scrapers to skin it, and needles and sinew to turn the hide into a warm coat to insulate their hairless bodies. As time went on, the clothes humans wore became an indicator of cultural and individual differences. Some were clearly developed to be more comfortable in the environment, others were designed for decorative, economic, political, and religious reasons.

Ritual costumes can tell us about the deities, ancestors, and civil and military ranking in a society, while other clothing styles can identify local or national identity. Social class, gender, age, economic status, climate, profession, and political persuasion are also reflected in clothing. Anthropologists have even tied changes in the hemline length of women's dresses to periods of cultural stress or relative calm.

In 13 beautifully illustrated volumes, the *Cultures and Costumes: Symbols of their Period* series explores the remarkable variety of costumes found around the world and through different eras. Each book shows how different societies have clothed themselves, revealing a wealth of diverse and sometimes mystifying explanations. Costume can be used as a social indicator by scientists, artists, cinematographers, historians, and designers—and also provide students with a better understanding of their own and other cultures.

ROBERT L. HUMPHREY, JR., Professor Emeritus of Anthropology,
George Washington University, Washington, D.C.

Ceremonial and Social Occasions

In bygone eras, pastimes were as much about show and display as pleasure and recreation. Clothes designed specifically for sports and leisure activities may be a product of the 20th century, but pastimes have had an impact on fashion throughout French history.

The tournament, one of the most colorful and exciting of medieval events, originated in northern France at the end of the 11th century. The earliest tournaments were more like battles than sporting events. Two groups of knights on horseback engaged in an organized, but savage, free-for-all, fighting the opposing team with all kinds of weapons. The winners took the armor and horses of the conquered knights, and demanded ransom payments for their safe return.

French kings and nobility quickly recognized the value of these recreational skirmishes as a source of trained knights for their armies. Rather than outlawing them, they established a few basic rules of engagement and organized

After the Revolution, people dressed more plainly and simply, abandoning many of the excessive fashions associated with the royal regime. Men wore somber tailcoats cut straight across the waist, while women wore high-waisted, white, cotton dresses.

Heraldry

During the 12th century, knights identified themselves in battle and at tournaments with bold, colorful designs. Each noble family used its own unique hereditary **emblem**, putting it on their shields and on the sleeveless **surcoats** they wore over their armor to dull the sun's rays. This is the origin of the phrase "coat-of-arms" for family signs. The study of coats-of-arms is called heraldry, after the officials known as heralds who recorded each family's emblem. Soon, armed followers were also wearing their noble employers' colorful emblems so people could easily see where their loyalties lay. These emblems quickly spread beyond their military origins. Noble families started authenticating documents by stamping their unique emblem in a shield shape onto melted wax. They identified their valuable possessions, such as silver, with these shields, and marked them on their donations to the church, such as stained-glass windows and **vestments**. They even used their unique shields to decorate their homes and tombs.

tournaments to test the knights' combat skills.

By the 14th century, contests known as jousts were replacing the team engagements popular in earlier tournaments. In a joust, a pair of knights fought each other on horseback with lance and shield.

Whereas tournaments were still dangerous, the jousting contests took greater account of the safety of the knights, who were needed for real battle. With rare exceptions, knights jousted with blunted weapons. Chain mail armor was replaced by tougher armor made from metal plate. Fifteenth-century knights began to fight with longer lances, made more effective by an innovative rest hook on their breastplate. Wooden safety barriers now separated jousting combatants, diminishing some of the danger of the contests. In addition, jousting knights wore protective frog-mouthed helmets, which were too heavy and cumbersome for real battles.

From their rough-and-ready origins, tournaments had developed into lavish spectacles by the 14th and 15th centuries. Spectators, dressed in their finery, enjoyed these great displays in comfort from luxurious covered stands. Over their armor, knights wore sleeveless surcoats sumptuously decorated with their own or their sponsor's colors and emblems. They covered their horses' body armor in similar ornate blankets. Some knights decorated their helmets with huge plumes in symbolic colors, such as blue and gold for the kings of France; while others wore a heraldic emblem, such as a swan or a horn, on top of their helmets.

By this time, successful knights were expected to combine courage with considerate behavior. They were both heroic warriors and polite gentlemen. The word *chivalrous*—meaning to have courteous manners, especially toward women—derives from the French term for the principles of knighthood. In fact, many a knight hoped to honor an important lady (a woman of superior social position) in the audience by winning a tournament contest.

When medieval ladies went to tournaments, they wore their most colorful outfits. Anything red was highly prized and quite expensive. Women's outer gowns, known as surcoats, were often sleeveless or sideless, revealing the long-sleeved tunics they wore underneath. Surcoats were embellished with decorative buttons, fur trim, and bands of jeweled embroidery. Around their waists, ladies wore belts, or **girdles**, often with a suspended purse. Another type of outer garment popular with ladies was the ***cotehardie***. This full-length gown, often worn without a girdle, was fitted down to the hips, but had a full skirt. The elegant simplicity of their gowns was a contrast to their extravagant headdresses and long, pointed shoes.

Court Balls

During the Renaissance, French royalty were famous for their magnificent court balls. Numerous painters captured this distinctive feature of French court life. Their artworks depict lively events in which ladies and gentlemen danced in their finest clothes. Athletic French dances, such as the *galliard*, which involved a series of fast steps and high jumps, were admired and copied throughout Europe. The emphasis was on fancy footwork because the bulky clothes fashionable at the time limited upper-body movement.

Sixteenth-century French ladies danced in gowns with immense padded sleeves and enormous skirts supported by a special petticoat known as a **farthingale**. Made with circular hoops of cane or whalebone, the farthingale was invented in Spain. The earliest farthingales were bell-shaped, but by the late 16th century, wheel-shaped farthingales, which originated in France, were popular across Europe. A close-fitting top set off the skirt's width.

By the mid-16th century, gowns were made in two separate parts. The upper part, called a bodice, was stiff through the torso and tapered at the waist.

Collars and Ruffs

Ladies' gowns were finished with a separate collar worn with low or high necklines. The dainty neck frill of the mid-16th century had become a cartwheel **ruff** by the end of the century. Collars were made of gauze and lace. Some were pleated and rolled into a figure-eight. There were also double ruffs composed of two layers of folded material, one above the other. Tinted starches colored the collars and helped them hold their stiff shape. At the French court, the collar tints had political significance, especially for Catholics and Protestants, who were battling for control of France at the time. Catholics used blue starch; Protestants used yellow. Sometimes, ruffs were so big they had to be supported by a wire frame at the back.

A fashionable couple dressed for a court ball, circa 1600. Her skirts are supported by wheel-shaped farthingales, a type of petticoat made with hoops. A special pendant that holds a solid ball of perfume called a pomander is suspended from her waist.

The bodice was attached to the lower skirt by hooks. Women often hid the join with a beautiful girdle.

French ladies often disguised themselves at a ball by wearing a mask. Thus disguised, a lady in a mask could flirt with handsome strangers while dancing. This accessory first became fashionable during the 16th century, and remained popular throughout the 17th and 18th centuries. Worn mainly by women, masks either hid the forehead and nose or covered the whole face. They were made of velvet, silk, satin, or soft leather. Masks not only concealed identity, but also offered protection from dirt and bad weather. They were worn on the busy city streets and on long journeys, as well as for spectacular court events.

Men went to a ball wearing their most extravagant outfits, made from the richest velvets, satins, and gold. Men's fashions in the 16th century showed off athletic physiques. Men dressed in padded **doublets** and skimpy trunk **hose** (a type of short **breeches**), which they wore with fitted stockings. It made them look a little like today's football quarterbacks.

Parisians strolling through the shopping galleries of the Palais Royal, circa 1620. Books are on sale, along with other luxury goods, such as fans, gloves, collars, muffs, and masks.

Gloves

Glamorous gloves were the ultimate status symbol. During the Middle Ages, most people, apart from the nobility and important churchmen, wore mittens. However, by the 17th century, gloves had become commonplace among the wealthier people.

The 17th-century glove flared at the wrist into a cuff called a gauntlet. Gloves were made of the finest leathers and beautifully embroidered, fringed, tasseled, and **scalloped**. Gold thread, precious gems, and pearls were used to decorate them. The most luxurious gloves were perfumed with musk, amber, and other exotic scents.

The Growth of the Middle Classes

During the early 17th century, as the middle classes grew more numerous and prosperous, shopping became a pastime in large urban centers like Paris. Colorful signboards and tradesmen's symbols identified the shops. Shops had a pair of horizontal shutters open to the street during the day, simultaneously allowing the customer to inspect the produce and the tradesman to display his skill. A tailor, for example, could clearly be seen cutting and sewing garments.

Larger towns had a variety of specialized markets—people who worked in certain trades, such as goldsmiths, tended to stick together in the same quarter.

Goods like books and fabrics were also sold from specialist market stalls, while street vendors sold everything from perfume to cakes.

Well-to-do men and women in the early 17th century wore colorful clothes. The French liked pale shades, such as sea green. They gave these colors bizarre names, such as "kiss me in love." Men dressed in matching jackets and breeches, with boots and a dashing feathered hat. Their jackets were worn open so people could see their white linen shirts. They finished their outfits with a falling lace collar and matching lace cuffs.

Winter Clothing

During the 1600s, Europe experienced exceptionally cold winters. Both men and women wrapped themselves in voluminous cloaks, which had been popular since pre-Roman days. Cloaks remained the outdoor garment of choice until the early 19th century. Seventeenth-century winter cloaks were ground-length and fastened at the neck with a cord. They were often lined with warm fur. Some people wore a short cape as well for extra protection against the cold. **Mufflers** and fur collars guarded the neck against the icy winds.

Men and women not only wore gloves in winter, but they also warmed their hands in muffs—short, padded tubes with side openings. Muffs were usually made of fur, but they also came in embroidered silk, velvet, and gold and silver cloth.

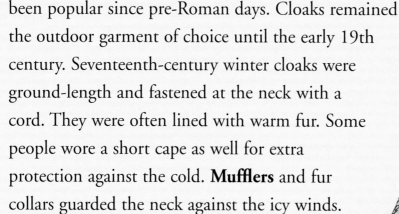

Ladies retained the fashion for puffy sleeves, but abandoned the farthingale. As a result, the profile was more natural-looking and relaxed. Early 17th-century gowns had high waists with full skirts. They were made of plain velvet, silk, or satin. A small selection of loops, bows, and **rosettes** were often used as decoration. At their necklines and wrists, women wore falling lace collars identical to the men's. Although lace caps were popular, women often went bareheaded. They wore their hair in ringlets with a knot at the back of the head.

Riding Habits

From the medieval period until the early 19th century, men rode horses wearing their boots and everyday clothes. However, women adopted distinctive riding **habits** much earlier.

During the 17th century, women rode on special **sidesaddles**, which accommodated their long gowns. Women's clothing had been elaborate and extravagant since the Renaissance. One of the earliest forms of sportswear, women's riding habits, evolved out of women's need for practical clothes.

The Duchesse de Bourgogne was married to Louis XIV's grandson. In this famous portrait by Pierre Gobert, she wears a riding habit based on fashionable men's clothes of the early 1700s.

Seventeenth-century women's riding habits were literally outfits with split personalities—women topped their skirts with more comfortable and practical menswear, adopting men's coats, vests, and **cravats**. Sometimes, they even wore men's wigs and hats when riding. Despite the gradual transformation of women's riding habits, the half-masculine, half-feminine look remained standard until women stopped riding sidesaddle in the early 20th century.

For wealthy French citizens of the 18th century, grooming and getting dressed in the morning was a social occasion. This woman's servant is arranging her hair while merchants show her the latest materials and a musician plays her tunes.

Good Grooming

For wealthy people in 18th-century France, getting dressed was a social occasion. Friends dropped by for a casual visit and to gossip about the previous night's events. They might stay and listen to musicians or look at goods that merchants had come by to show.

Personal grooming was a time-consuming business. Several servants were employed just to help wealthy people to "arrange their **toilet**" (perform their grooming regime). Both men and women often wore heavy makeup, such as powder, rouge, and **beauty patches**. People did not bathe all that often in the 18th century, which led to skin problems, and these were often worsened by the white lead in many of their cosmetics. Wealthy people either wore a wig or curled their hair with a curling iron. Hairstyles were finished with white powder and **pomade** to hold them in place. Women, and sometimes men, narrowed their waists with **corsets**. Women also put on **panniers** to hold out their skirts.

Both sexes wore dressing gowns while arranging their toilet. These loose, comfortable garments had been fashionable for relaxing at home since the late 17th century. Unlike modern examples, 18th-century dressing gowns were luxurious, showy garments worn in front of other people. Women's dressing gowns were more delicate then men's and were trimmed with lace and ruffles.

Liberté, Egalité, Fraternité

During the French Revolution, fashion's excesses became a symbol of aristocratic tyranny and decadence. Citizens rejected clothes that emphasized the distinctions between different classes. They soon discarded corsets, panniers, wigs, high heels, powder, beauty patches, and ribbons. Instead of reflecting rank and status, clothes, they felt, should express equality. Women wore their hair in simple knots and dressed in plain white cotton gowns. Men's clothes became somber. They took off their wigs and wore their hair short. Revolutionary fervor urged a return to classical purity.

Military and Men's Costumes

From the late Middle Ages to the French Revolution, men's and women's fashions were equally extravagant. The simplicity of today's menswear is largely a 19th-century invention, led by British fashions. Before 1800, richly decorated clothes reflected a man's importance and position in society.

From the 11th to the 13th centuries, soldiers' armor was made of chain mail: thousands of little metal rings linked together to form protective garments. It was used for shirts, mittens, hose, and hoods. Chain mail garments weighed a lot, but they were flexible enough not to be too uncomfortable.

The 14th century saw a transition from chain mail to articulated plate armor. This type of armor was made from sheets of tempered steel formed into specific parts: breastplates, back plates, and collar plates, fastened together with flexible joints. Each plate of armor was made to the wearer's exact proportions. Armorers molded helmets and visors to the precise shape of the wearer's head and face.

Noblemen of the late medieval era attend a banquet. Some are dressed in articulated armor while others wear short doublets and hose. Two men at the table are wearing tall, brimless sugarloaf hats.

The 14th century was a transitional period in armor design. This medieval knight wears a chain mail shirt and articulated plate armor on his legs and arms so that his entire boy is completely covered.

By the 15th century, suits of plate covered the entire body from head to toe. Armor became so heavy that knights needed help just to mount their horses. Foot soldiers, by contrast, began wearing less armor because it affected their mobility so much. Men gradually stopped wearing metal armor in the 16th century because it offered little protection against a new weapon deployed on the battlefield—the musket, or gun.

Undergarments

Under his chain mail or plate armor, a soldier traditionally wore a fitted and padded tunic made of thick cloth or leather. By the 16th century, this tunic had become a kind of coatdress for men called a doublet. Worn with a shirt underneath, doublets varied from knee- to hip-length and were extremely padded and puffed. Men wore doublets with trunk hose—short, full **knickerbockers**—which were equally padded and puffed, with fitted waistbands and thigh bands, and which looked a little like pincushions. In the second half of the 16th century, men started wearing tightly fitted, knee-length breeches called cannons under their trunk hose. And last, they wore netherstocks, a type of stocking pulled up over the cannontops.

Chevaliers

In the late 16th century, France was plunged into a religious war between Catholics and Protestants. The French royal army was in turmoil. Except for the occasional breast plate, soldiers rarely wore armor. Infantry (foot soldiers) wore thick, cotton padding under their doublets instead. Uniforms were scarce, which meant French troops were colorful, if nothing else.

Chevaliers, the swashbuckling knights on horseback of the early 17th century, always had a sword ready at their side just in case they needed to defend themselves. These adventurers dressed in flamboyant style, with matching jackets and breeches in colorful shades, like ice blue, canary yellow, or pink. They wore their long hair in ringlets and waves. They tossed their cloaks casually over their shoulders, and on their heads wore dramatic hats with long plumes.

Boots played a major role in a *chevalier's* outfit. In the first half of the 17th century, they were an important fashion statement for men. They were worn on every occasion, both indoors and outdoors, and were a must for men on horseback.

Fashionable boots had soft funnel tops, high heels, platform soles, and square toes. These boots creased and sagged on the calves. A wide, bow-like flap covered the instep and was held in place by a strap fastened under the boot. In town, men turned the funnel down, creating the bucket shape typical of the era. On horseback, men turned the funnels up and covered their knees.

This late 16th-century man wears a padded doublet with padded breeches. His outfit is accessorized with a ruff around his neck and a short cape.

During the 16th and 17th centuries, soldiers gradually stopped wearing armor because it could not protect them against a new weapon deployed on the battlefield—the musket, or gun.

In the 17th century, knights wore a type of special sock called boot hose with their boots. Originally, they protected expensive silk stockings from wear and tear. However, once funnel-top boots became fashionable, boot hose acquired fancy edges with lace, ruffles, or fringe loops, which cascaded over the boot tops. Soon, boot hose became a luxury item in its own right, often decorated with gold and silver lace and embroidery.

Military uniforms evolved gradually over the 16th and 17th centuries from the **liveries** worn by armed retainers and servants of the nobility during the medieval era.

The French Guard

Ever since 1563, the soldiers who guarded the king were known as the French Guard. They were renowned for their extravagant dress, especially for formal occasions. Under Louis XIV, France was constantly engaged in bloody conflicts, and a young man was considered privileged to begin his military career with light duties in the king's household.

By the 1660s, the French Guard had a recognizable uniform, although there were slight variations from company to company. Officers wore scarlet uniforms trimmed with silver **brocade**, while their men dressed in gray. By the 1690s, their uniforms had developed more of a military look.

The king's troop consisted of three companies: guards, household cavalry, and musketeers. In addition, by the 1720s, there were 59 cavalry regiments in France. Cavalrymen (soldiers on horseback) carried a sword, a musket, and pistols. They wore their sword on a strap of white or yellow hide. They dressed in leather breeches and wore thick, strong boots, and used cloaks to keep out the cold. In addition, their horses' saddles and blankets bore the personal symbols and colors of the colonel of the regiment.

Throughout the 18th century, French military uniforms gradually became less individualisitc and more consistent in style. Blue and red were the king's colors. The French Guards wore a blue coat, a red vest underneath, and red stockings. Most soldiers wore wigs with their uniforms, even though they were unhygenic and could be very uncomfortable.

By the 1780s, **epaulets** decorated with fringe had become part of the French Guard's uniform. Together with the red vest and blue coat, officers now wore white breeches and a smaller, neater version of the tricorne (three-cornered) hat.

The Jackboot and *Justaucorps*

During the late 17th and early 18th centuries, the jackboot entered the wardrobe of riders and military men. It was made of hard "jack," a type of leather stiffened by coating it with boiling pitch (tar). This heavy boot had square toes, chunky square heels, and a funnel top that covered the knee. In the 18th century, the back part was often cut out to make it easier to bend the knees. Bootmakers also produced a more flexible, light-weight jackboot without an instep flap.

Around the same time, the coat began to replace the doublet, which had been customary menswear for the last two centuries. This coat, known as the *justaucorps*, originated in France in about 1665 to 1670. At first, the coat was a loose, flared garment, cut just above the knee, its front edges turned back and elaborately decorated. Its sleeves were cut just above the wrist and ended in big cuffs. Under their coats, men wore a shirt. Tied around their throats, was a cravat, a lace-edged length of white linen or **lawn**. The combination of coat and breeches put the boot out of fashion, except for traveling and bad weather—men now wore shoes with buckles.

The coat of choice for the next hundred years, the *justaucorps* eventually settled into its classic appearance. By the 1680s, it was knee-length and fitted at the waist. There were buttons and buttonholes from neck to knee, but fashionable men only buttoned their waist buttons. Buttons and buttonholes were often trimmed with gold and silver braid and embroidery. There was no collar to get in the way of the curls of the **periwig**. Sleeves were now full-length, ending in huge turned-back cuffs decorated with buttons and embroidery. A richly trimmed sword sash was often slung across the body. Toward 1700, the *justaucorps* became even more fitted at the waist, and its skirt fuller and flared.

Habit à la Français

The basic 18th-century outfit for men was known as *habit à la français*. All but the very poorest wore this throughout the 18th century. It was a three-piece costume, consisting of a *justaucorps* coat, vest, and breeches. However, this suit was not necessarily made in matching colors or fabric. The coat was knee-length, fitted, and flared out from the waist, while the vest and knee-length breeches were fitted. The breeches were worn with hose and shoes. A shirt with frilly cuffs was worn next to the skin. The outfit was finished with a cravat and tricorne hat. As the century

This man from the 1680s is dressed in an early form of the tricorne hat and the *justaucorps* coat. Under his hat, he wears a long, curly periwig.

progressed, this suit became slimmer and plainer, with a somber, streamlined profile. At first, this outfit was made in bright, gaudy colors, but gradually, it became darker and less richly ornamented. As the wearing of swords declined steadily throughout the 18th century, it became fashionable for men to carry a short cane or walking stick.

Overcoats

Men and women did not start wearing heavy overcoats outdoors until the 18th century. Up until then, they wrapped themselves in cloaks in bad weather. The earliest overcoats were similar to regular coats—fitted to the waist, then flared to knee-length. The only significant difference was the heavier material they were made of, adding an extra layer of protection on top of the regular coat.

Decadents and Dandies

A dandy was originally a man excessively concerned with fashion. Eighteenth-century dandies wore an exaggerated form of the dress of the day. They had clothes made of more extravagant fabrics and in outrageous colors. While an average man's clothes became more somber, dandies liked stripes. They dressed with exquisite care and attention to detail. Their coats were shorter and even tighter than the norm, and were cut away in a sloping manner, to be worn open. Their breeches were skintight, with ribbon loops at the knee. They completed the whole effect with a miniature tricorne hat, either held in the hand or perched on an extravagantly high wig.

Other 18th-century designs were based on the coats of coachmen, who drove in the open through every kind of weather, from wind to snow. Coachmen kept warm in heavy-duty greatcoats, overcoats that were cut long and full. They were **double-breasted** with a big collar, and often had one or more shoulder capes for additional protection against the cold. Men started wearing overcoats for traveling and riding. The French *redingote*, or riding coat, was one such design.

The National Assembly abolished the distinct uniforms of various regiments during the French Revolution. Republican soldiers now dressed in blue coats and put tricolor cockades in their hats showing support for the Revolutionary cause.

Fashionable from the 1720s onward, it was long and made of thick cloth. The *redingote* had a large, turned-back collar and cuffs. Just like other greatcoats of the time, they were double-breasted and had short shoulder capes. This coat was first introduced for women in the 1780s. The ladies' version was full-length and made of lighter-weight fabric. It was high-waisted and fitted through the torso, just like contemporary gowns, then cut away to reveal the dress underneath.

Post-Revolution

After the French Revolution, the National Assembly abolished the provincial and foreign names of regiments and anything distinct about the color and decoration of army uniforms. Republican soldiers dressed in blue coats. However, red and white trim was still used to distinguish rank or position, such as drummer boy. A red, white, and blue **cockade** showing support for the revolutionary cause was an obligatory addition to the hats of republican soldiers, who no longer wore wigs. Instead, they powdered and pomaded their own hair and wore it tied back in a pony tail or in braids.

After the Revolution, men's clothes started to look like modern men's formalwear. Men now looked to England for direction in fashion, and wore **tailcoats**, cut straight in front at the waist to reveal the vest below. Knee breeches and stockings were going out of fashion—except for formal occasions—increasingly replaced with trousers. A cravat, gloves, cane, and top hat completed the outfit. There was now a tendency to cut trousers and coats from the same material. Fabrics were plain, and colors were somber. Men's hair was cut short, left in natural curls and waves, and combed forward over the forehead and ears.

The Influence of the Court

Renowned for its luxurious splendor, the French court set the pace for European clothing right up until the Revolution. It was the desire of the French court for more and more stupendous clothing that originally put Paris on the fashion map.

The nobility and other wealthy people had looked to the French court for fashion direction since medieval times. Diplomats picked up ideas from other courts and brought them home. The spread of pictures, prints, and pamphlets, which flourished in the Renaissance, helped spread new ideas in fashion.

Events in the king's life, such as his birthday, were marked with mass celebrations. These events were often recorded for posterity in pictures, as well as by word of mouth, all of which carried the king's name, fame, and reputation for magnificent clothes far afield.

Royal **coronations**, weddings, and funerals all involved immense preparation and ceremony. They were on a huge scale, combining the

Louis XIV loved splendor and had a great influence over new fashions. This scene depicts him receiving vistors, there on official business, in his elaborate bedchamber. At this stage, Louis did not wear a wig.

production values of today's Olympic Games, a Broadway show, and Oscar night all rolled into one. The most magnificent festivities in all of 17th-century Europe accompanied the coronation of the French king at Rheims and the burial of the Duke of Lorraine at Nancy.

Royalty also toured the country, for both tactical and practical reasons. They wanted to keep nobles and people who worked for them on their toes. Processions of all kinds—religious and civic, as well as royal—were displays of unity and order, as well as visual feasts of splendid garments.

Until the 14th and 15th centuries, the nobility dressed in a similar style to the people they ruled. The main differences were the quality of the materials used and the richness of the decoration. The clothes of the nobility were trimmed with sumptuous embroidery, gold, silver, and jewels. The line between everyday clothes and clothes for formal occasions

became increasingly blurred as the nobility began to dress in finery all the time.

Wearing Fur

Furs had a special place in the fashion of the Middle Ages. The richest nobles wore **sable** and **ermine**, while humbler folk had to make do with rabbit and squirrel fur. However, by the mid-16th century, furs were losing out to richer fabrics as status symbols. One result of this was that the vocabulary for grades and types of furs became increasingly rich—and open to misinterpretation. When the fairy tale *Cinderella* was translated from its original French in the 17th century, Cinders' slippers, which were lined with *vair* ("squirrel fur"), became—most improbably—slippers of *verre* ("glass").

The coronation of Marie de Médici, the wife of King Henri IV, was a magnificent spectacle. Ruffs had reached their high point in 1575, and by 1610, they had been replaced by large, fan-shaped collars.

The Color of Money

Wearing certain colors was a way of displaying conspicuous wealth and status. Some dyes, like purple, were difficult to make and therefore quite expensive. That made them all the more desirable to the heads of some noble families, who expressed their preferences for them in no uncertain terms. Amadeus VI and Amadeus VII of Savoy were called, respectively, the Green Count and the Red Count, because they only wore these costly colors.

In the 12th and 13th centuries, upper-class gentlemen liked dressing in tunics decorated with their family colors and heraldic symbols. At the time, French kings and their family often wore azure (blue) robes decorated with golden *fleurs-de-lis*. According to legend, this ancient emblem was based on the iris flower. Azure garments, especially cloaks, decorated with golden *fleurs-de-lis* became traditional for the coronation of French kings. Family colors and heraldic symbols could also be worn by upper-class ladies, but only if they were married.

A married lady typically wore clothes with decoration divided down the middle lengthwise. On one side was her family's coat of arms, and on the other side was her husband's. However, the vogue for this type of clothing gradually died out once armed retainers and servants began wearing livery decorated with the noble family's emblem.

Oriental Influences: New Fabrics and Rich Patterns

A new status symbol soon came along: exotic and extremely expensive fabrics imported from the East. Damask is a richly decorated fabric with a figured pattern that is part of the weave. It is named for Damascus, the Middle Eastern city where this beautiful silk was originally woven. Taffeta, a fine, crisp silk with a

This medieval woman is a member of the French royal family. She wears an azure blue gown decorated with golden *fleur-de-lis* and lavishly trimmed with ermine.

glossy iridescent sheen, was introduced from Persia (present-day Iran). Velvet, a closely woven, originally silk fabric with a short, dense pile, like shorn fur, came from the Orient.

The court of the dukes of Burgundy possessed the most beautiful fabrics of all. Rich in design and color, Burgundian dress was admired, copied, and envied by the whole of Europe, especially in the 15th century. It was noted for the richness of its patterned fabrics, gold and silver cloth, and jeweled embroideries; its materials were generously edged and lined with costly furs.

It was also admired for its extreme elegance of style. Copying a fashion started at the Burgundian court in the 14th and 15th centuries, European men shaved off their beards and cut their hair short, turning it under all around. The Burgundian men also started a fashion for wearing a doublet in a carelessly stylish way, open to the waist so that their shirts showed underneath. The short doublet rapidly replaced the long tunic, which until that time had been the mainstay garment of the nobility. Burgundians wore colored or striped stockings. The feet of the hose were padded and had leather soles, dispensing with the need for shoes except in bad weather, when boots were worn.

Separating the Rich from the Poor

In the 14th century, the nobility began differentiating themselves from the people they ruled, not only by using fine materials, but also by cutting and styling their clothes in fancy and innovative ways. The Renaissance nobility had a decided taste for political ostentation, propaganda, and display. They encouraged a policy of calculated grandeur in the representation of royalty. Monarchs not only dressed differently from their subjects, they engaged in rituals that set them apart.

The details of a costume could establish a person's rank, and there were strict rules about who could and could not wear certain colors and jewels. In most European countries, there were "sumptuary laws" that dictated what a

The Sun King

Louis XIV, who was called the Sun King, loved ceremony and dressing up. As a young man, he reportedly went to court functions in clothes covered with so much gold embroidery that "neither the stuff nor the color could be seen." He used such displays to symbolize his personal power as absolute monarch.

During his 54-year reign, Louis lived in the public glare at the pinnacle of a magnificent court. Versailles was the center of a kind of theater-state in which the main actor was the monarch himself. The way of life in the palace—an ostentatiously large household—celebrated even the most mundane details of the king's daily life, including the routines of getting up, eating meals, and going to bed. The nobles and rival monarchs were quick to emulate every one of these details as a statement of their own power. Louis XIV's ever-present sun motif in the decoration at Versailles symbolized the glorious Sun King radiating power and vision.

person could and could not wear. These laws covered the choice of materials—chosen to encourage the growth of national industries—and the display of jewelry and color—to prevent the lower classes from imitating the nobility.

The Court of Louis XIV

During the late 17th century, French noblemen at the court of Louis XIV wore such tall periwigs that they had to carry their large tricorne hats in their hands.

The noblemen's immense wigs were echoed by the towering headdresses of French noblewomen. Ladies at Versailles wore the tall, curly *fontange* with feathers, ribbons, or precious stones attached. *Fontanges* were made of starched and fluted rolls of fabric held in place by wires, and they could be up to two feet (60 cm) tall.

In the 1690s, stylish ladies at Versailles wore a *fontange*, a tall lacy headdress introduced by Louis XIV's mistress, Mademoiselle de Fontanges. It rapidly became popular among wealthy women.

Noblewomen's gowns were as extreme as their headdresses. The bodice was stiff and fitted, tapering sharply just below the waist. The overskirt was drawn back and fell in heavy folds to the back or sometimes to one side. The heavy underskirt was decorated with rich embroidery, a large frill, or tassels. In fact, the gown was often laden with so many strips of gold brocade that it became almost too heavy to walk in comfortably. Shoes had high heels for added stature.

The court of Louis XIV started a fashion for *justaucorp* coats for men. These were made of extravagant materials, beautifully trimmed with gold braid and jeweled buttons. They were worn with petticoat breeches or *rhinegraves*. This unusual male fashion took the form of a knee-length skirt, like a Scottish kilt, or a knee-length skirt-shorts combination. Petticoat breeches were trimmed all over with ribbon loops, bows, and lace ruffles.

18th-Century Courtiers

During the 18th century, the French court continued to be a center of conspicuous consumption and display, famous throughout Europe for its glamour and excess. The *levée*, the regal ceremony of getting up each morning, is a perfect example of ritual display. In this daily routine, the king was accompanied by dozens of **courtiers**, from the highest minister to the humblest shirt holder. The courtiers took all of this quite seriously and jostled for status and precedence within this **sycophantic** world. Every member of court had his own mini-household modeled on the king's, with the number of liveried servants and the splendor of the attire giving a fair indication of his status. The influence of such customs extended beyond Versailles to wealthy society in general.

Women started wearing a new type of gown at court. It had a fitted waist in the front, but flowed loosely over a pair of panniers, large, basket-like structures sticking out at the back and sides. A pannier, which means "basket" in French, was made from hoops linked with panels of cloth, like a petticoat, and tied on at the waist. Worn under a dress, they gave an exaggerated fullness below the waist.

The neckline on these gowns was low and wide, and the bodice was flat in front and decorated with dozens of bows. Ladies wore a special neck cloth called a *fichu* to cover their dramatically plunging necklines. Sleeves were elbow-length in a layered style.

By about 1730, the gown had evolved into a garment known as a *robe à la française*. In this style, the front of the bodice was fitted, but

A noblewoman in formal court dress of the 1770s. She wears enormous skirts held out by a pair of basket-like panniers tied around her waist underneath her gown, and a towering wig.

the back was designed in the shape of a large box that extended from neckline to hem. Sleeves ended in a cuff at the elbow, below which hung the lace flounces of the **chemise**. Despite its departure from the pannier shape in mid-century, the *robe à la française* continued to be fashionable until the 1770s, when it was reserved for formal court wear.

Versailles remained an important cultural model until the French Revolution (1789–1799), but the more worldly urban culture of well-to-do Parisians became increasingly influential. Fashions changed dramatically, especially after the Revolution.

Gowns no longer came in separate bodice and skirt parts. They were extremely plain and made of muslin with *fichus* of white cotton instead of silk and brocade. The long gloves of silk or fine leather were replaced by the less-elegant half-gloves of cotton, net, or lace.

Fashions were given new patriotic names, such as *Constitution* or *Camille*. Tricolor themes were also used to decorate dresses. Rosettes on belts and plumes on hats were colored red, white, and blue. The *negligée à la patriote* for ladies consisted of a royal blue *redingote* and a white dress with a red-and-white striped collar.

War and Peace

During the years of the Revolution, many dressmakers and tailors who had once worked for the aristocracy closed their shops and fled or went into hiding. Their absence led eventually to another—albeit minor—revolution in Paris. The first shops selling ready-made dresses opened and quickly spread to other parts of Europe.

Later, Napoleon returned the nation to stability. His priorities may have been empire-building and politics, but his powerful image and the new elite at court brought a luxurious simplicity and splendor to the world of fashion. Their efforts to stimulate the economy helped restart this famous French industry and put Paris back in the fashion business.

The Importance of Headdress

The lavishness of French court dress was matched only by the extravagance of court headdress, which was widely copied throughout Europe. Every trend—from the sugarloaf hats of the 14th century to Marie Antoinette's high wigs of the 1770s—had a major impact on contemporary fashion.

During the Middle Ages, most men wore hoods, caps, or close-fitting bonnets tied under the chin. Women covered their heads with veils secured with pins or a ribbon or metal band. The **wimple** is the best known of all medieval headdresses for women. This popular headdress completely framed the face. It consisted of a veil, usually white, pinned beneath the face from ear to ear to cover the neck, and another veil that covered the head. The bottom of the wimple was tucked into the gown's neckline.

From the 13th century onward, women started wearing net caps called cauls. They were made of colored cord or gold and silver thread. Some cauls had jewels at the seams. Cauls ranged from soft, round cases for braids to

Women in spectacular headdresses from the Middle Ages, including a wimple (far left), a steeple headdress (second from right), and two variations of braids in a caul.

dramatic headdresses like horns. The more extreme designs were attached to a rigid metal framework.

During the 14th and 15th centuries, headdresses were influenced by styles brought back to Europe by crusaders and merchants from the Middle East. A wealthy lady might wear a colorful veil fixed with a jeweled **brooch** to a turban studded with gems, or a miter-shaped headdress in golden brocade. A variant of this headdress dipped in the center and had a rose at the sides. It was made of a padded roll covered in velvet or silk and decorated with pearls and jewels.

Marie de Clèves launched a fashion in France for the steeple headdress: a cone-like hat with a transparent veil hung from the tip. The veil was often made of gold threads and artfully arranged on wires so that it stood out like butterfly wings. This headdress grew to such proportions that ladies had to twist their heads sideways to get through doorways. Some people believe architects enlarged the entrances to the Castle of Bois just for the sake of this fashion. In fact, steeple headdresses became so enormous that a law was passed in France restricting their use to the most important aristocracy. As a result, a shortened version became popular toward the end of the 15th century.

During the 16th century, women's headdresses became less grandiose and included the horseshoe-shaped hood (far left) and a hood with shoulder flaps (far right).

Men's Headdress

During the 14th century, the points on men's hoods grew until they hung down the wearer's back like a tail. These special points were called **liripipes**. The *chaperon* was a new type of headdress, evolved from a man's hood and shoulder cape. Men had begun draping the cape in attractive folds on their heads when

A woman sits at a dressing table, arranging her hair into fashionable ringlets with a curling iron, circa 1620.

they did not want to wear it on their shoulders. By the 15th century, it was no longer necessary to re-drape the materials each time the hood was put on. A padded roll was added, and the shoulder cape was sewn on one side and the liripipe on the other. This new headdress was made of rich fabrics and often decorated with jeweled brooches. It resembled a turban and remained fashionable until the early 16th century.

Burgundian noblemen introduced another popular 15th-century men's headdress. This tall hat resembled a sugarloaf.

In the 16th century, men cut their hair short and wore beards. Black or dark caps were enormously popular. Their upturned edges were sometimes **slashed** (designed with slits that revealed a contrasting fabric underneath) and decorated with cords or ribbons. The finest examples were made of velvet and ornamented with jeweled brooches and plumes. In the second half of the 16th century, hats with tall crowns and narrow brims also became fashionable. They were made of black felt or velvet and decorated with a wavy plume. Men wore these hats at an angle on the head.

In the first half of the 16th century, elaborate hoods replaced headdresses as the headcovering of choice for women. Designs were simple, usually black caps with hanging ends and back, worn over white headscarves. The flaps fell upon the shoulders and at the back was a semicircular piece of material hanging in folds. A horseshoe-shaped hood, which originated at the French court, became popular in the late 1520s and '30s. It was placed farther back on the head so that a central hair parting could show. The hood was made from a wide band of fabric supported by one or two metal bands that were sometimes decorated with jewels. A long hood hung in folds behind the bands and down the back. Toward the middle of the 16th century, French hoods were slightly flattened on top.

During the mid-16th century, caps also became fashionable for women. They sat on the crown of the head so women's hair could be seen. Wealthy women's caps were made of black velvet and decorated with slashing, jewels, and plumes similar to the men's.

Since hats were a must on formal occasions, men often carried them in their hands because their periwigs were so tall. The floppy hats of the early 17th century became more structured. The brim was turned back and the round crown lowered so that hats could easily be tucked under the arm. This evolved into the tricorne hat, which had numerous variations.

By the 18th century, the tricorne was the most popular choice for men. Its only serious rival was the flatter, bicorne (two-cornered) hat, invented in the latter half of the 18th century. In France, it was called the *chapeau bras* and was a great favorite with Napoleon.

Beauty Patches

In the 17th and 18th centuries, fashionable men and women put beauty patches on their faces. These were made of little pieces of black silk or velvet cut into different shapes, such as circles, stars, crescents, moons, and hearts. In France, they were called *mouches* (meaning "flies"). The placement of patches could have special meanings; for example, one near the mouth meant the wearer was feeling flirtatious. However, most people wore beauty patches to disguise major skin blemishes. They stored them in pretty little boxes with separate compartments for the glue and brushes needed to put them on.

Men's Caps and Dressing Gowns

To accommodate their heavy periwigs, men cropped their hair short or shaved their heads. However, bare heads were considered undignified, so men covered them up while relaxing at home with caps made from silk, velvet, or fur.

Seventeenth-century men's caps were often decorated with lavish embroidery. Some men preferred the more exotic look of an Oriental-style turban.

When they were not wearing their wigs, men put on more casual and comfortable dressing gowns. Men had relaxed in long, open coats since the 16th century. In the early 17th century, a new type of dressing gown imported from India became fashionable. Known as a *banyan*, it was more fitted than 16th-century examples. *Banyans* were made of Indian silk and cotton and printed with attractive stripes or patterns. By the late 17th century, these dressing gowns were being made in Europe from any luxurious material, from velvet to satin.

Hairstyles and Wigs

Toward the end of the 16th century, women often left their heads uncovered because they wore such enormous **ruffs**. Women's hair was padded and puffed just like their clothes. It was set in lots of tiny curls, which were then piled high on the head. Alternatively, women wore their long hair swept up without a parting. Pads were often used to increase the height of the hairstyle. Some women resorted to wigs to achieve this look. Hair was decorated with plumes, strands of pearls, jewels, and ribbons.

Fashions relaxed and became more natural-looking by the 1620s. Men had large mustaches and tiny pointy beards. They grew their hair to shoulder length and curled it in soft waves. They topped their luxuriant locks with floppy, wide-brimmed hats with long, fluffy plumes. Women wore their hair in ringlets with coiled braids or a large knot at the back of the head. Hairstyles were accented with flowers, strands of pearls, or bits of lace. Although women often went bareheaded, they also wore caps and bonnets. These were nearly always plain white, but decorated with lace, embroidery, pleating, ruffled edges, and ribbons.

Wigs were the primary headcovering for men in the latter half of the 17th century. According to legend, once Louis XIV started disguising his thinning hair with a wig, the fashion quickly spread across Europe. Known as periwigs, they came in natural colors, from black to blond. The best wigs were made of human hair, and French wigmakers were the most renowned in Europe. In fact, French wigs were in such demand that Colbert, the minister of finance, imposed an export duty on them. At first, periwigs were fairly natural-looking, with gentle, shoulder-length waves. However, by the 1680s, they had grown to enormous proportions, with masses of cascading curls that peaked on either side of a central parting.

During the second half of the 16th century, women wore their ringlets longer and frizzier. Hairstyles were wired to look wider and fuller at the sides. The most popular ladies' headdress of the era was a *fontange*, named for

Mademoiselle de Fontanges, Louis XIV's mistress. This stiff, towering confection had a wire frame and was covered in silk and linen. It was decorated with a profusion of lace **flutes** and ribbon loops with long streamers down the back. The *fontange* carried an echo of men's tall periwigs.

The long, curly periwig remained popular until around 1715. After that time, a smaller, tied-back style with fluffy temple waves came into fashion for men. The ponytail part of the wig was called a *queue* in France. At about the same time, men started whitening their wigs with powder. By the mid-18th century, men's wigs had become more formal. Hair was swept neatly back from the forehead and arranged in uniform "sausage" curls at the sides. The majority of men continued to wear wigs until the French Revolution.

In the early part of the 18th century, women wore a neat, unparted hairstyle with simple curls at the back. After around 1740, they began arranging their hair with side curls. The compact look was disappearing, and hair was swept up in taller styles. Women began to powder their hair white and used pomade to keep it in place. They swept their hair up over pads to create larger and larger styles. For evening and formal occasions, they added false corkscrew curls and put flowers and plumes in their hair. By the end of the 1760s, hairstyles were towering, and it became easier for most fashionable women to wear wigs to achieve this look.

If the 18th century was the era of the tricorne hat for men, then it was the era of the cap for women. Most ladies wore them in one form or another, especially indoors. Caps from the first half of the 18th century were small and had streamers at the back. They were worn perched on top of the head. As hairstyles grew larger and more elaborate in the second half of the 18th century, so did the caps that had to accommodate them. Some were tied under the chin with big bows, while others, like the frilly butterfly cap, had no fastenings.

Marie Antoinette promoted the enormous wigs of the 1770s in France. Their foundations were padded and wired to give them support. Some

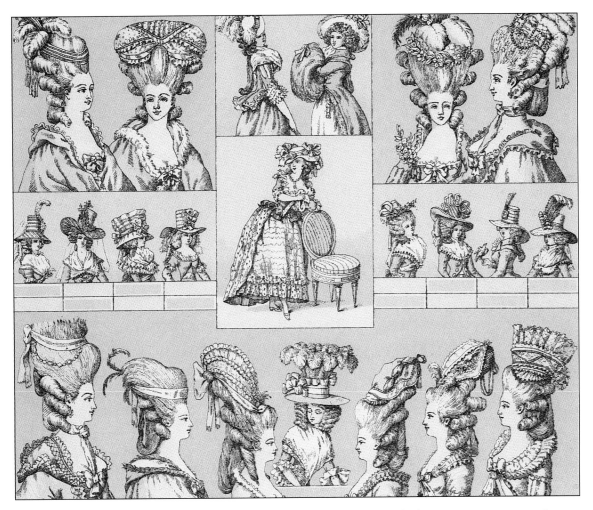

Women wearing the enormous powdered wigs with huge sausage curls, popular in the 1770s. These wigs had padded and wired foundations to support their extreme heights.

were more than three feet (90 cm) tall. Hair ornaments could be equally excessive—a ship or miniature garden scene was a favorite among a stylish minority.

However, by the 1780s, women's hair had returned to a less extreme style. Some women did away with wigs and powder altogether. As they diminished in height, hairstyles increased in width. Hair was frizzed at the sides and covered the ears. This new look was called the hedgehog style, and it was worn with a wide-brimmed picture hat.

The Lower Classes, Trades, and Provincial Variations

Despite France's reputation as a leading trendsetter, some people working in certain professions or trades or living in the countryside dressed in fashions that had not changed much since the medieval era.

Church **vestments** have their origin in the Middle Ages. The most important of these is a large, semicircular cloak worn by senior priests. Known as a cope, this cloak was worn only in ceremonial processions. The priests wore a full, sleeveless outer vestment called a chasuble while celebrating Mass. Chasubles were often made of fine materials enhanced with decorative embroidery.

A French middle-class family during the Revolutionary era. Note the cockades in the men's hats and the patriotic red, white, and blue prints on the women's skirts.

A priest celebrating Mass carried in his left hand an embroidered towel called a maniple, originally used for wiping wine from the gold or silver goblet, called a chalice.

Beneath the chasuble, priests wore a long white robe called an alb. All Church officials wore the alb, not just priests. The albs of priests and higher Church dignitaries were decorated with six panels of ornament attached to the breast, the back, each cuff, and the front and back of the foot of the garment. A deacon assisting at Mass wore a silk upper tunic called a dalmatic over his alb. A subdeacon wore a linen tunic over his alb. Both of these were shorter than the alb. Dalmatics and tunics worn by bishops and abbots were edged with a fringe.

Senior churchmen also wore a floor-length, embroidered stole, which passed around the neck and crossed over the chest and was held in place by a girdle at the waist. Archbishops and bishops wore a tall, pointed headdress called a miter, which was often decorated with gold and jewels. On their shoulders, archbishops wore a symbol of office that came from the Pope. This narrow white band was known as a pallium. Richly decorated gloves and slippers were also part of the archbishop's outfit.

Monks, Friars, and Nuns

Abbeys, monasteries, and convents played an important role in French society. They offered education, gave aid to the poor, looked after the sick, and gave hospitality to travelers. Most of these religious communities were founded in the Middle Ages as a place where men and women could devote themselves to God.

The distinctive habits of medieval monks, friars, and nuns have not changed much since those times. These simple, uniform-like garments are a sign of humility before the Lord and symbolize a lack of interest in worldly matters. Religious habits were made of simple, sometimes rough, fabrics. They came in somber shades, like brown, black, gray, and dark blue. Colors depended on which religious order the person belonged to. Augustinian friars,

A group of medieval church dignitaries in albs with various vestments on top. The priest in the center is dressed in a cape, while the priests beside him wear chasubles to celebrate Mass.

for example, wore white habits. Monks wore long robes, which they belted with a piece of rope; the robes had hoods called cowls. They either went barefoot or wore sandals. Monks had a special haircut called a tonsure, in which the hair on the tops of their heads was shaved, but was left ear-length at the sides. In medieval times, priests wore their hair in the same way. Nuns covered themselves fully from head to toe. They wore wimple headdresses and stark, floor-length gowns with sandals or plain slippers.

In many ways, academic dress is similar to church vestments. This is because the Church originally set up and ran the schools and universities. On ceremonial occasions, professors and scholars still dress in gowns and hoods. The three ranks of scholar—bachelor, master, and doctor—are distinguished by slight differences in the gowns.

The graduate's mortarboard is another product of the medieval era. This unusual head covering derives from a headdress worn by men at the University of Paris in the early 16th century. Known in French as the *bonnet carré*, the fashion soon spread across Europe. The early form was a soft, flat, square cap worn on top of a skullcap. In the early 17th century, the two parts were joined to one another and the flat, square part was stiffened into a board to keep the corner from flopping over the face. By the mid-17th century, the center **boss** had appeared, and a tassel was attached to this in the 18th century. The medieval influence persists today in other professions. French lawyers and judges dress in distinctive black gowns and tall, rounded hats based on medieval dress.

Peasants and Workers

Until the 14th century, what differentiated the clothes of the nobility from those of the peasantry was the quality of material or the richness of decoration.

Medieval peasants dressed in simple knee-length tunics and fitted hose. They wore straw hats to keep the sun's rays off their heads while working in the fields.

The nobility wore clothes made of silks, velvet, and fur, whereas craftspeople and peasants wore simpler homespun materials in colors like brown, blue, and white.

Craftsmen and male peasants dressed in tunics, usually knee-length, with tight-fitting hose. They tied a cord around the hips, from which hung a square bag for carrying tools or other items. Sometimes, a piece of cloth was tied around the waist and used to carry bread. Men wore a hood, and women tied bonnets on their heads.

Women wore loose-fitting gowns with tight sleeves, and under their gowns they wore a tunic. The top gown was sometimes hitched up to keep it clean and to show off the garment beneath. Throughout the Middle Ages, women grew

Wedding Dress

Surprisingly, the traditional "white wedding" does not have medieval origins. It is an invention of the late 18th and early 19th centuries. During the medieval era, there were no specific bridal colors or clothes. There are plenty of pictures of medieval brides in red, green, or blue gowns. Medieval bridal outfits were merely more stylish and luxurious than everyday clothes. Just how stylish and opulent the gown was depended on the social position and wealth of the bride. Nevertheless, by the end of the 16th century, brides were wearing white to represent their virginity and innocence. From this time onward, brides dressed in white as a sign of purity.

In the second half of the 18th century, royalty and nobility made it stylish to get married in white or silver. By the late 18th century, white gowns inspired by the robes on classical statues were the height of fashion. All these trends gradually came together in the early 1800s to make white a must for brides. However, the bridal veil did not become fashionable for another 20 years.

their hair long, but covered it up with veils or hoods. Peasants of both sexes often wore a straw hat over their headdress while working in the fields.

The Rise of the Middle Classes

As some town-dwelling merchants and artisans grew wealthier in the late Middle Ages and Renaissance, they could afford better-quality clothes. They began to recognize dressing up as the great source of pleasure and confidence that we still enjoy today.

Naturally, they wanted sumptuous materials cut in the latest style. During these times, fashionable and luxurious clothing was seen as an expression of power and wealth. Feeling threatened by the new trend, the noble establishment constantly sought to pass sumptuary laws, which restricted the types of clothing worn by the various levels of society. However, people worked out ways to get around these laws, which, in any case, were difficult to enforce.

The world changed dramatically between the Renaissance and the 19th century. New continents were discovered beyond Europe. There was a boom in international commerce. Communication, which had gradually improved due primarily, in part, to the invention of the printing press in 1450, now opened up dramatically. By the mid-18th century, the Industrial Revolution was in full swing in England, where it had begun.

Yet France remained primarily an **agrarian** society. Twenty million peasants—about three-quarters of the population of France—owned only about one-third of the land. The rest belonged to the Church, the bourgeoisie (middle classes), and the nobility. There was not enough land to go around, and many lived in abject poverty. There was a severe economic downturn in the 1770s, as wages were not keeping pace with prices, and the state was almost bankrupt. France was set firmly on the road to revolution.

Revolutionaries

Sans-culottes was the name given by French aristocrats to working-class revolutionaries from Paris, because they wore trousers, not fashionable breeches. The term literally means "without breeches." The *sans-culottes* dressed in ankle-length trousers with an extra panel buttoned on at the front just like a sailor's pants. Their trousers were usually cut from red and white striped material. This was topped with a short woolen jacket with two pockets and a wide collar with red lapels. *Sans-culottes* wore wooden clogs or went barefoot. Despite their name, the

A country wedding during the reign of Louis XIII (1610–1643). At the time, there were no specific bridal colors or clothes. Brides like this woman in the center merely wore dressier and more luxurious outfits.

most important part of their outfit was a red knitted cap with a turned-up brim and a long tassel hanging down the back. Immensely popular with working men, this *bonnet rouge* became a potent symbol of liberty. The female counterparts of the *sans-culottes* dressed in simple colored gowns that flared at the waist. They wore white caps on their heads and *fichu* scarves tied around their necks.

Regional Differences

Of course, some parts of provincial France were relatively isolated. Four-fifths of French men and women found marriage partners within 15 miles of their village birthplace. In many areas, people spoke Breton, German, Spanish, Basque, or any one of numerous dialects. French was a minority language in France, especially

Marie Antoinette as Milkmaid

Louis XVI and his Austrian wife, Marie Antoinette, were cushioned from the day-to-day grind of working-class French lives by luxury. Although royal outlay actually accounted for a only a tiny proportion of state expenditure, extravagance had always been part of the French court's image. The king and queen were widely blamed for all of France's difficulties. To add insult to injury, the frivolous queen had developed a passion for getting back to nature. She created a rural playground hamlet—the Petit Trianon—at Versailles, where she dressed up as a milkmaid. Her costume was a highly idealized version of clothes worn by women who sold milk on the streets. She dressed in an ankle-length gown hitched up at the sides, which kept it clean and also let her pretty petticoat show. The whole effect was completed by a white apron and lace cap.

among the peasantry. Even by the 1790s, one in four could not speak a word of French, and many more could not hold a complex conversation in the language.

Not only did these people speak a different language, but they also had unique customs and clothes that go back to medieval times and the Renaissance era.

In the Mâcon and Bresse regions, in eastern central France, women wore the most extraordinary broad, flat hats. These were decorated with long pieces of black lace and tied under the chin. A gold tassel hung over the brim, and the back of the hat was covered with a long piece of black lace. Another variation of this headdress was a lace bonnet held in place by two ribbons. One was tied under the chin, and another tied around the back of the head and draped down the back. Over this, women of these regions wore a spool-like black headdress decorated with pleated black lace.

In Alsace, near the present-day border with Germany, women wore a tall headdress rather like a bishop's miter, known as a *bendel*. In Normandy, women wore white veils arranged like a butterfly's wings.

To this day, the people of Brittany—a large, isolated peninsula on the Atlantic coast—are well known for their traditional dress, which they still wear. Breton women wore dresses fitted through the torso, flared at the waist, and cut wide at the neck. Under this was a tight-fitting shirt with a wide collar that covered the shoulders. Sometimes, Breton women wore a jacket over their dresses, and decorative, embroidered aprons were a popular accessory. On their heads, women wore headdresses decorated with lace and ribbons, called *coifs*. Usually white, styles varied from wimple-like veils to lofty bonnets, according to district or town.

Breton men dressed in short, blue jackets, breeches, and boots. They wore shirts with a wide collar and a vest that reached the neckline and crossed over to fasten on one side. Their vests had two rows of brass buttons and were trimmed with black velvet or embroidery borders. They wore broad, flat hats and sashes or belts with fancy buckles around their waists. Both men and women from Brittany wore clothes decorated with traditional embroidery in red, yellow, green, and white. Their Sunday-best clothes were even more ornate.

Glossary

Note: Specialized words relating to clothing are explained within the text, but those that appear more than once are listed below for easy reference.

Agrarian relating to fields or farming

Beauty patch a tiny piece of black silk or court plaster worn on the face or neck especially by women to hide a blemish or to heighten beauty

Boss a raised ornamentation

Breeches short pants covering the hips and thighs and fitting snugly at the lower edges at or just below the knee

Brocade a fabric characterized by raised designs

Brooch an ornament that is secured on a garment by a pin or clasp

Chemise a loose, straight-hanging dress

Cockade an ornament usually worn on a hat as a badge

Corset a close-fitting supporting undergarment that is often hooked and laced and that extends from above or beneath the bust or from the waist to below the hips

Courtier a person in attendance at the royal court

Cravat a scarf or tie

Double-breasted having one half of the front lapped over the other and usually a double row of buttons and single row of buttonholes

Doublet a close-fitting jacket worn by men

Ermine white, winter fur of the weasel-like animal of the same name

Farthingale a support of hoops worn beneath a skirt to expand it at the hipline

Fontange a tall, late 17th-century ladies' headdress decorated with lace curls and ribbon loops

Flute a grooved pleat

Girdle belt or sash

Habit a costume worn for horse riding, or garments worn by churchpeople

Hose a cloth leg covering that sometimes covers the foot

Knickerbockers loose-fitting short pants gathered at the knee

Lawn a fine sheer linen or cotton fabric of plain weave

Livery the distinctive clothing or badge formerly worn by the retainers of a person of rank

Muffler a scarf

Pannier an overskirt draped at the sides of a skirt for an effect of fullness

Periwigs wigs with long, cascading curls worn by men in the 17th and early 18th centuries

Pomade a fragrant hair dressing

Rosette an ornament usually made of material gathered or pleated so as to resemble a rose and worn as a badge of office

Ruff a large round collar of pleated muslin or linen

Scalloped a pattern consisting of a continuous series of circle segments or angular projections forming a border

Sidesaddle a saddle used by women wearing a long skirt whose design lets them sit with both legs on the same side of the horse

Sycophantic relating to self-seeking flattery towards another person

Vestment garment worn at church ceremonies by religious officials

Timeline

1337–1443	The Hundred Years War between England and France.
1348	Bubonic plague leads to huge population losses.
1431	Joan of Arc is burned at the stake.
1464	The king of France establishes a postal system.
1470	The first printing presses in France are established in Paris.
1494–1559	Italian Wars: France and Austria fight over Italian territories.
1515	François I is crowned king.

1519	Leonardo da Vinci dies in the arms of François I.
1534	Jacques Cartier leads an expedition to Canada.
1547–1559	The reign of Henri II.
1562–1598	The Wars of Religion.
1572	The massacre of Protestants on St. Bartholomew's Eve in Paris.
1589–1593	Henri IV becomes the first Bourbon king and converts to Catholicism, ending the Wars of Religion.
1608	The founding of Quebec.
1617	Louis XIII is crowned at the age of 17.
1624	Richelieu enters the royal council as principal minister (to 1642).
1631	A French newspaper carries the first classified ads.
1642	Blaise Pascal invents the pascaline, an automatic calculator.
1643	Louis XIV becomes king, with Mazarin as principal minister.
1682	The royal court moves to Versailles.
1685	Louis XIV revokes the Edict of Nantes.
1715	Louis XIV dies and Louis XV accedes.
1762	Rousseau's *Social Contract* is published.
1769	Napoleon Bonaparte is born in Ajaccio, Corsica.
1774	Louis XVI becomes king.
1778–83	France supports the American Revolution.
1789	The French Revolution and the storming of the Bastille (July 14).
1792	Louis XVI is tried for treason and convicted; the monarchy is abolished.
1793	Louis XVI and Queen Marie Antoinette are guillotined in Paris.
1794	Robespierre is overthrown; the end of the Reign of Terror.
1796	Napoleon weds Rose de Beauharnais (the future Empress Josephine).
1799	General Bonaparte enters Paris crowned emperor; creation of the First Empire.

Online Sources

La Courturiére Parisienne Costume and Fashion
www.marquise.de
Part of the Costume Ring created to link sites dedicated to costume and its history. Plenty of beautiful contemporary illustrations from medieval to the 20th century.

France.com
www.france.com/culture/renaissance.html
This wide-ranging site gives a useful profile of France and its social customs; French history; and architecture, from prehistoric times to the 20th century.

Creating French Culture
http://www.loc.gov/exhibits/bnf/
This online exhibition was developed by the Library of Congress. It is an introduction to French history lavishly illustrated with treasures from the Bibliothèque Nationale de France.

French Art History
http://www.uncg.edu/rom/courses/dafein/civ/art.html
This University of North Carolina site features French art from prehistoric to modern times and provides background information on French history and culture, including timelines.

Heraldica
www.heraldica.org
This site offers information on all aspects of French heraldry from titles, coronets, crests, mottoes, the arms of France, and the French flag, to a genealogy of the French royal family and Napoleonic titles

The Costume Page
http://members.aol.com/nebula5/costume.html
A library of costume and costuming-related links with over 2,000 links listed on these pages.

Further Reading

Aston, Margaret, ed. *The Panorama of the Renaissance.* London: Thames and Hudson, 1996.

Cobbs, Richard, and Colin Jones, eds. *The French Revolution: Voices from a Momentous Epoch 1789–1795.* London: Simon and Schuster, 1988.

De Pietri, Stephen et al. *New Look You: French Haute Couture 1947–1987.* Chicago: Rizzoli, 2001.

Jones, Colin. *Cambridge Illustrated History of France.* Cambridge: Cambridge University Press, 1994.

Kelly, Francis M. and Randolph Schwabe. *European Costume and Fashion 1490–1790.* Mineola, NY: Dover, 2002.

Olien, Joanne (ed.). *Parisian Fashion of the Teens: 352 Elegant Costumes from L'Art et la Mode.* Mineola, NY: Dover, 2002.

Reeves, Compton. *Pleasures and Pastimes in Medieval England.* London: Sutton Publishing, 1997.

Sichel, Marion. *History of Women's Costume.* London: Batsford Academic and Educational, 1984.

About the Author

Alycen Mitchell writes and lectures on the decorative arts, specializing in jewelry and fashion. She grew up in Canada and now lives with her partner in the U.K. She has worked in both the antique business and fashion retailing and holds an MA in 19th-century art and design from the University of London. As an author, she has contributed to many publications from *The Financial Post* and *Management Consultancy* to *Antique Dealer* and *Collectors Guide* and the art and antiques Web site www.icollector.com.

Index